The Treasure Map

Explorer Challenge

Find out what is in the sea
at the top of the map ...

OXFORD
UNIVERSITY PRESS

The children were counting their steps.
"We are making a map of the garden,"
Biff told Mum.

They went inside to draw the map.
Suddenly the key began to glow.

The magic took them to an island with palm trees and golden beaches.

"Look," said Anneena. She pointed at a tall ship. "That's a pirate ship!" said Biff. "Hide!"

It was too late. The pirates were already on the island.

"Are you looking for Big Jim's treasure?"
demanded the captain.
"No!" said Chip. "Who's Big Jim?"

"Big Jim is a pirate, too," said the captain. "He stole the king's treasure and hid it on this island."

The captain grinned.
"*I* stole Big Jim's map!" he said. "Now you can help us find the treasure."

The captain looked at the map.
"Next we must go to the trees at
the east side of the island," he said.

At the trees, he said, "The treasure is twenty steps north of the red rock."

After twenty steps, the pirates gave
the children spades.
"Start digging!" ordered the captain.

The children dug and dug. It was
hard work in the hot sun.

"There is no treasure," said Chip.
The captain was not happy.

"Wait!" said Anneena. "How tall was Big Jim?"
The captain held one hand up high.

"Big Jim must have long legs," explained Anneena. "His steps will be much longer!"

The pirates counted twenty
long steps from the red rock.

This time the children quickly
found the treasure chest.

The key was glowing.
"Why did you help the pirates, Anneena?"
asked Biff.

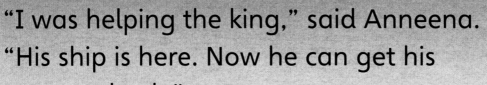

"I was helping the king," said Anneena. "His ship is here. Now he can get his treasure back."

At home, the children measured the garden again.
"This time we are using a tape measure," Biff told Mum.

Retell the Story

Look at the pictures and retell the story in your own words.

Look Back, Explorers

 Who stole Big Jim's map?

 Where did they find the treasure chest?

 Why did Biff say they would use a tape measure?

 Why is Jim called Big Jim?

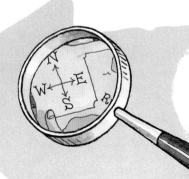  Did you find out what is in the sea at the top of the map?

Explorer Challenge: blue rock island (page 11)

What's Next, Explorers?

Now you have read about the pirates using a map to find treasure, find out about how to use maps and compasses ...

Map, Compass, Explore!

Catherine Baker
Series created by Roderick Hunt and Alex Brychta

OXFORD

Explorer Challenge
for *Map, Compass, Explore!*

Find out what this means on a compass ...